# This Journal Belongs to:

| Date: | Time: |

| Deck: | Type of Spread: |

## Question

## Interpretation

## Notes

| Date: | Time: |

| Deck: | Type of Spread: |

## Question

## Interpretation

## Notes

| Date: | Time: |
| Deck: | Type of Spread: |

## Question

## Interpretation

## Notes

| Date: | Time: |
| Deck: | Type of Spread: |

## Question

## Interpretation

## Notes

<table>
<tr><td>Date:</td><td>Time:</td></tr>
<tr><td>Deck:</td><td>Type of Spread:</td></tr>
</table>

## Question

## Interpretation

## Notes

Date:

Time:

Deck:

Type of Spread:

Question

Interpretation

Notes

Date:
Time:
Deck:
Type of Spread:
Question
Interpretation
Notes

Date:

Time:

Deck:

Type of Spread:

## Question

## Interpretation

## Notes

| Date: | Time: |
| --- | --- |
| Deck: | Type of Spread: |

## Question

## Interpretation

## Notes

<table><tr><td>Date:</td><td>Time:</td></tr><tr><td>Deck:</td><td>Type of Spread:</td></tr></table>

## Question

## Interpretation

## Notes

## Question

## Interpretation

## Notes

Date:

Time:

Deck:

Type of Spread:

## Question

## Interpretation

## Notes

| Date: | Time: |
| Deck: | Type of Spread: |

## Question

## Interpretation

## Notes

**Date:** | **Time:**

**Deck:** | **Type of Spread:**

## Question

## Interpretation

## Notes

Date: | Time:
Deck: | Type of Spread:

## Question

## Interpretation

## Notes

| Date: | Time: |
| Deck: | Type of Spread: |

## Question

## Interpretation

## Notes

| Date: | Time: |

| Deck: | Type of Spread: |

## Question

## Interpretation

## Notes

| Date: | Time: |

| Deck: | Type of Spread: |

## Question

## Interpretation

## Notes

| Date: | Time: |
| Deck: | Type of Spread: |

## Question

## Interpretation

## Notes

## Question

## Interpretation

## Notes

| Date: | Time: |
| Deck: | Type of Spread: |

## Question

## Interpretation

## Notes

## Question

## Interpretation

## Notes

<table>
<tr><td>Date:</td><td>Time:</td></tr>
<tr><td>Deck:</td><td>Type of Spread:</td></tr>
</table>

## Question

## Interpretation

## Notes

| Date: | Time: |
| Deck: | Type of Spread: |

## Question

## Interpretation

## Notes

| Date: | Time: |

| Deck: | Type of Spread: |

## Question

## Interpretation

## Notes

**Date:**                **Time:**

**Deck:**              **Type of Spread:**

## Question

## Interpretation

## Notes

## Question

## Interpretation

## Notes

| Date: | Time: |

| Deck: | Type of Spread: |

## Question

## Interpretation

## Notes

| Date: | Time: |
| Deck: | Type of Spread: |

## Question

## Interpretation

## Notes

| Date: | Time: |

| Deck: | Type of Spread: |

## Question

## Interpretation

## Notes

| Date: | Time: |
| Deck: | Type of Spread: |

## Question

## Interpretation

## Notes

| Date: | Time: |
| Deck: | Type of Spread: |

## Question

## Interpretation

## Notes

| Date: | Time: |

| Deck: | Type of Spread: |

## Question

## Interpretation

## Notes

**Date:** | **Time:**

**Deck:** | **Type of Spread:**

## Question

## Interpretation

## Notes

**Date:**        **Time:**

**Deck:**        **Type of Spread:**

## Question

## Interpretation

## Notes

| Date: | Time: |
| Deck: | Type of Spread: |

## Question

## Interpretation

## Notes

| Date: | Time: |

| Deck: | Type of Spread: |

## Question

## Interpretation

## Notes

| Date: | Time: |
| Deck: | Type of Spread: |

## Question

## Interpretation

## Notes

**Date:** **Time:**

**Deck:** **Type of Spread:**

## Question

## Interpretation

## Notes

| Date: | Time: |
|---|---|
| Deck: | Type of Spread: |

## Question

## Interpretation

## Notes

**Date:**

**Time:**

**Deck:**

**Type of Spread:**

## Question

## Interpretation

## Notes

Date:
Time:
Deck:
Type of Spread:

## Question

## Interpretation

## Notes

**Date:** | **Time:**

**Deck:** | **Type of Spread:**

## Question

## Interpretation

## Notes

| Date: | Time: |

| Deck: | Type of Spread: |

## Question

## Interpretation

## Notes

| Date: | Time: |

| Deck: | Type of Spread: |

## Question

## Interpretation

## Notes

Date:

Time:

Deck:

Type of Spread:

## Question

## Interpretation

## Notes

Date: | Time:

Deck: | Type of Spread:

## Question

## Interpretation

## Notes

| Date: | Time: |
| Deck: | Type of Spread: |

## Question

## Interpretation

## Notes

**Date:**

**Time:**

**Deck:**

**Type of Spread:**

## Question

## Interpretation

## Notes

Date: Time:

Deck: Type of Spread:

## Question

## Interpretation

## Notes

| Date: | Time: |
| Deck: | Type of Spread: |

## Question

## Interpretation

## Notes

| Date: | Time: |
| Deck: | Type of Spread: |

## Question

## Interpretation

## Notes

| Date: | Time: |

| Deck: | Type of Spread: |

## Question

## Interpretation

## Notes

| Date: | Time: |
| Deck: | Type of Spread: |

## Question

## Interpretation

## Notes

| Date: | Time: |

| Deck: | Type of Spread: |

## Question

## Interpretation

## Notes

<table><tr><td>Date:</td><td>Time:</td></tr><tr><td>Deck:</td><td>Type of Spread:</td></tr></table>

## Question

## Interpretation

## Notes

<table><tr><td>Date:</td><td>Time:</td></tr><tr><td>Deck:</td><td>Type of Spread:</td></tr></table>

## Question

## Interpretation

## Notes

| Date: | Time: |
| Deck: | Type of Spread: |

## Question

## Interpretation

## Notes

Date:
Time:
Deck:
Type of Spread:

## Question

## Interpretation

## Notes

| Date: | Time: |

| Deck: | Type of Spread: |

## Question

## Interpretation

## Notes

| Date: | Time: |
| Deck: | Type of Spread: |

## Question

## Interpretation

## Notes

| Date: | Time: |
| Deck: | Type of Spread: |

## Question

## Interpretation

## Notes

| Date: | Time: |

| Deck: | Type of Spread: |

## Question

## Interpretation

## Notes

| Date: | Time: |
| Deck: | Type of Spread: |

## Question

## Interpretation

## Notes

| Date: | Time: |
| Deck: | Type of Spread: |

## Question

## Interpretation

## Notes

## Question

## Interpretation

## Notes

| Date: | Time: |
| Deck: | Type of Spread: |

## Question

## Interpretation

## Notes

| Date: | Time: |

| Deck: | Type of Spread: |

## Question

## Interpretation

## Notes

# Date:     Time:

# Deck:     Type of Spread:

## Question

## Interpretation

## Notes

| Date: | Time: |
| Deck: | Type of Spread: |

## Question

## Interpretation

## Notes

| Date: | Time: |
| Deck: | Type of Spread: |

## Question

## Interpretation

## Notes

| Date: | Time: |

| Deck: | Type of Spread: |

## Question

## Interpretation

## Notes

| Date: | Time: |
| Deck: | Type of Spread: |

## Question

## Interpretation

## Notes

| Date: | Time: |

| Deck: | Type of Spread: |

## Question

## Interpretation

## Notes

<table><tr><td>Date:</td><td>Time:</td></tr><tr><td>Deck:</td><td>Type of Spread:</td></tr></table>

## Question

## Interpretation

## Notes

| Date: | Time: |
| Deck: | Type of Spread: |

## Question

## Interpretation

## Notes

| Date: | Time: |
| Deck: | Type of Spread: |

## Question

## Interpretation

## Notes

Date: Time:

Deck: Type of Spread:

## Question

## Interpretation

## Notes

| Date: | Time: |

| Deck: | Type of Spread: |

## Question

## Interpretation

## Notes

| Date: | Time: |

| Deck: | Type of Spread: |

## Question

## Interpretation

## Notes

<table><tr><td>Date:</td><td>Time:</td></tr><tr><td>Deck:</td><td>Type of Spread:</td></tr></table>

## Question

## Interpretation

## Notes

| Date: | Time: |

| Deck: | Type of Spread: |

## Question

## Interpretation

## Notes

**Date:**  **Time:**

**Deck:**  **Type of Spread:**

## Question

## Interpretation

## Notes

| Date: | Time: |

| Deck: | Type of Spread: |

## Question

## Interpretation

## Notes

| Date: | Time: |
| Deck: | Type of Spread: |

## Question

## Interpretation

## Notes

| Date: | Time: |
| Deck: | Type of Spread: |

## Question

## Interpretation

## Notes

| Date: | Time: |
| Deck: | Type of Spread: |

## Question

## Interpretation

## Notes

| Date: | Time: |

Deck: | Type of Spread:

## Question

## Interpretation

## Notes

| Date: | Time: |
| Deck: | Type of Spread: |

## Question

## Interpretation

## Notes

| Date: | Time: |
| Deck: | Type of Spread: |

## Question

## Interpretation

## Notes

<table>
<tr><td>Date:</td><td>Time:</td></tr>
<tr><td>Deck:</td><td>Type of Spread:</td></tr>
</table>

## Question

## Interpretation

## Notes

<table><tr><td>Date:</td><td>Time:</td></tr><tr><td>Deck:</td><td>Type of Spread:</td></tr></table>

## Question

## Interpretation

## Notes

| Date: | Time: |
| Deck: | Type of Spread: |

## Question

## Interpretation

## Notes

| Date: | Time: |
| Deck: | Type of Spread: |

## Question

## Interpretation

## Notes

| Date: | Time: |
| --- | --- |
| Deck: | Type of Spread: |

## Question

## Interpretation

## Notes

| Date: | Time: |
| Deck: | Type of Spread: |

## Question

## Interpretation

## Notes

Date: | Time:

Deck: | Type of Spread:

## Question

## Interpretation

## Notes

| Date: | Time: |
| Deck: | Type of Spread: |

## Question

## Interpretation

## Notes

| Date: | Time: |

| Deck: | Type of Spread: |

## Question

## Interpretation

## Notes

| Date: | Time: |
| Deck: | Type of Spread: |

## Question

## Interpretation

## Notes

| Date: | Time: |

| Deck: | Type of Spread: |

## Question

## Interpretation

## Notes

| Date: | Time: |
| Deck: | Type of Spread: |

## Question

## Interpretation

## Notes

| Date: | Time: |

| Deck: | Type of Spread: |

## Question

## Interpretation

## Notes

Date: Time:

Deck: Type of Spread:

## Question

## Interpretation

## Notes

| Date: | Time: |

| Deck: | Type of Spread: |

## Question

## Interpretation

## Notes

| Date: | Time: |
|---|---|
| Deck: | Type of Spread: |

## Question

## Interpretation

## Notes

| Date: | Time: |

| Deck: | Type of Spread: |

## Question

## Interpretation

## Notes

## Question

## Interpretation

## Notes

| Date: | Time: |

| Deck: | Type of Spread: |

## Question

## Interpretation

## Notes

**Date:**

**Time:**

**Deck:**

**Type of Spread:**

## Question

## Interpretation

## Notes

| Date: | Time: |
| Deck: | Type of Spread: |

## Question

## Interpretation

## Notes

<table>
<tr><td>Date:</td><td>Time:</td></tr>
<tr><td>Deck:</td><td>Type of Spread:</td></tr>
</table>

## Question

## Interpretation

## Notes

# Date: | Time:

# Deck: | Type of Spread:

## Question

## Interpretation

## Notes

Date:

Time:

Deck:

Type of Spread:

## Question

## Interpretation

## Notes

<table><tr><td>Date:</td><td>Time:</td></tr><tr><td>Deck:</td><td>Type of Spread:</td></tr></table>

## Question

## Interpretation

## Notes

| Date: | Time: |
|---|---|
| Deck: | Type of Spread: |

## Question

## Interpretation

## Notes